# Pebble™

## First Biographies
# Marian Anderson

## by Eric Braun

**Consulting Editor:** Gail Saunders-Smith, PhD
**Consultant:** Nancy M. Shawcross, Curator of Manuscripts
Rare Book and Manuscript Library
University of Pennsylvania

Capstone
press
Mankato, Minnesota

Pebble Books are published by Capstone Press,
151 Good Counsel Drive, P.O. Box 669, Mankato, Minnesota 56002.
www.capstonepress.com

1  2  3  4  5  6  10  09  08  07  06  05

*Library of Congress Cataloging-in-Publication Data*
Braun, Eric, 1971–
    Marian Anderson / by Eric Braun.
    p. cm.—(Pebble Books. First biographies)
    Includes bibliographical references (p. 23) and index.
    ISBN 0-7368-4232-2 (hardcover)
    1. Anderson, Marian, 1897–1993—Juvenile literature. 2. Contraltos—United
States—Biography—Juvenile literature. 3. African American singers—Biography—
Juvenile literature. I. Title. II. Series: First biographies (Mankato, Minn.)
ML3930.A5B73 2006
782.1'092—dc22                                               2004028521

Summary: Simple text and photographs present the life of singer Marian Anderson
and her famous concert at the Lincoln Memorial.

## Note to Parents and Teachers

The First Biographies set supports national history standards for units on people and culture. This book describes and illustrates the life of Marian Anderson. The images support early readers in understanding the text. The repetition of words and phrases helps early readers learn new words. This book also introduces early readers to subject-specific vocabulary words, which are defined in the Glossary section. Early readers may need assistance to read some words and to use the Table of Contents, Glossary, Read More, Internet Sites, and Index sections of the book.

# Table of Contents

## Time Line

1897
born

# Young Marian

Marian Anderson was born in Philadelphia in 1897. Marian loved to sing as a child. Everyone said she had a beautiful voice.

## Time Line

1897
born

1914
begins private
voice lessons

Marian wanted to be a better singer. At age 17, she tried to go to music school. But the school would not teach black people. Marian took private voice lessons instead.

Popular Benefit Concert

TO ASSIST IN MUSICAL EDUCATION OF
Miss MARION E. ANDERSON
Musical Fund Hall        June 23rd, 1915
AUSPICES PEOPLE'S CHORAL SOCIETY
ALFRED J. HILL, Director
S. BLANCHE POOLE, Accompanist

WILLIAM L. KING, Accompanist

# Time Line

1897
born

1914
begins private
voice lessons

Marian practiced hard.

Her voice grew stronger.

She gave concerts at

music halls and churches.

Many people came

to hear her sing.

Musical Fund Hall, where Marian sang to help pay for
her lessons; advertisement for one of her concerts (inset)

## Time Line

1897
born

1914
begins private
voice lessons

1925
wins singing
contest

# Professional Singer

In 1925, Marian won a singing contest. The prize was to sing with a large orchestra in New York City. The concert was a success. Marian was becoming famous.

◄ Marian at age 28

## Time Line

1897
born

1914
begins private
voice lessons

1925
wins singing
contest

1927
goes to
Europe

Two years later, Marian went to a music school in Europe. She practiced hard to learn new songs. Marian became one of the best singers in the world.

◄ Marian working with a music teacher in Europe in 1931

## Time Line

| 1897 born | 1914 begins private voice lessons | 1925 wins singing contest | 1927 goes to Europe |

# Voice of Change

In 1939, Marian wanted to sing at Constitution Hall in Washington, D.C. But the owners had rules against black people. They would not let Marian sing there.

Constitution Hall around 1939

## Time Line

1897
born

1914
begins private
voice lessons

1925
wins singing
contest

1927
goes to
Europe

Marian did not show anger at the unfair rules. She sang at the Lincoln Memorial instead. Millions of people heard her sing on the radio. Many people loved her songs.

1939
sings at Lincoln
Memorial

## Time Line

| | | | |
|---|---|---|---|
| 1897 born | 1914 begins private voice lessons | 1925 wins singing contest | 1927 goes to Europe |

In 1955, Marian sang at the Metropolitan Opera in New York City. She was the first black person to sing at this famous opera house.

◀ Marian getting ready to sing at the Metropolitan Opera

1939
sings at Lincoln Memorial

1955
sings at the Metropolitan Opera

## Time Line

| 1897 | 1914 | 1925 | 1927 |
| born | begins private voice lessons | wins singing contest | goes to Europe |

In 1965, Marian gave her final concert at Carnegie Hall. She spent the rest of her life helping poor people. She died in 1993. Today, people remember Marian for her beautiful voice.

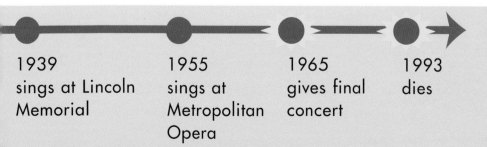

1939
sings at Lincoln Memorial

1955
sings at Metropolitan Opera

1965
gives final concert

1993
dies

# Glossary

**Carnegie Hall**—a famous concert hall in New York City

**concert**—a show given by a singer or musician

**contest**—an event in which people compete for a prize

**Lincoln Memorial**—a large statue in Washington, D.C., that honors President Abraham Lincoln

**opera house**—a building where singers perform a musical play

**orchestra**—a large group of musicians who perform together, usually including string, wind, and percussion instruments

**private lessons**—meetings at which a teacher teaches skills to just one student

# Read More

**McKissack, Pat, and Fredrick McKissack.** *Marian Anderson: A Great Singer.* Great African Americans. Berkeley Heights, N.J.: Enslow, 2001.

**Meadows, James.** *Marian Anderson.* Journey to Freedom. Chanhassen, Minn.: Child's World, 2002.

**Ryan, Pam Muñoz.** *When Marian Sang: The True Recital of Marian Anderson, the Voice of a Century.* New York: Scholastic, 2002.

# Internet Sites

FactHound offers a safe, fun way to find Internet sites related to this book. All of the sites on FactHound have been researched by our staff.

Here's how:

1. Visit *www.facthound.com*
2. Type in this special code **0736842322** for age-appropriate sites. Or enter a search word related to this book for a more general search.
3. Click on the **Fetch It** button.

FactHound will fetch the best sites for you!

# Index

Word Count: 246
Grades: 1–2
Early-Intervention Level: 18

**Editorial Credits**

Aaron Sautter, editor; Heather Kindseth, set designer; Patrick D. Dentinger, book designer; Kelly Garvin, photo researcher/photo editor

**Photo Credits**

Corbis/Bettmann, cover
Getty Images Inc./Hulton Archive/Metronome, 1; Time Life Pictures/ Thomas D. Mcavoy, 14, 16
Marian Anderson Collection, Rare Book and Manuscript Library, University of Pennsylvania, 4, 6, 8 (both), 10, 12, 18, 20